INSIDER'S GUIDE TO

GERMAN 'DOLLY' COLLECTING
Girl Bisque Dolls
by Jan Foulke
Photographs by Howard Foulke

Buying, Selling & C

Published by Hobby H , nc.
Grantsville, aryland 21536

Other Titles by Author:

Blue Book of Dolls & Values®
2nd Blue Book of Dolls & Values®
3rd Blue Book of Dolls & Values®
4th Blue Book of Dolls & Values®
5th Blue Book of Dolls & Values®
6th Blue Book of Dolls & Values®
7th Blue Book of Dolls & Values®
8th Blue Book of Dolls & Values®
9th Blue Book of Dolls & Values®
10th Blue Book of Dolls & Values®
11th Blue Book of Dolls & Values®
12th Blue Book of Dolls & Values®

Focusing on Effanbee Composition Dolls
Focusing on Treasury of
Mme. Alexander Dolls
Focusing on Gebrüder Heubach Dolls
Kestner: King of Dollmakers
Simon & Halbig Dolls: The Artful Aspect
Doll Classics
Focusing on Dolls
Doll Buying & Selling Dolls
China Doll Collecting

COVER: 23in (58cm) Gebrüder Kuhnlenz 44. *H & J Foulke, Inc.* 18in (46cm) Simon & Halbig 949, open mouth with square teeth. *H & J Foulke, Inc.*

TITLE PAGE: This 24in (61cm) doll is a large and outstanding example of mold 143, a particular favorite of Kestner collectors. *H & J Foulke, Inc.*

BACK COVER: This large 25in (64cm) Handwerck is from seldom-found mold 199. She has a lovely, wistful expression on her face. *H & J Foulke, Inc.*

ADDITIONAL COPIES AVAILABLE @ **$9.95 plus postage**
FROM
HOBBY HOUSE PRESS, INC.
ONE CORPORATE DRIVE
GRANTSVILLE, MD 21536
1-800-554-1447

© 1995 by Jan and Howard Foulke

Printed in the United States of America

ISBN: 0-87588-443-1

TABLE OF CONTENTS
Questions from Collectors – **Answers from an Insider**

A Little History 5

The Dolly Face 16

What Is Bisque? 17

The Bodies..18

The Marks 21

The Dolls..24

Alt, Beck & Gottschalck 24
Bähr & Pröschild.........................26
C. M. Bergmann 30
Cuno & Otto Dressel....................32
Heinrich Handwerck...................35
Max Handwerck 38
Karl Hartmann 40
Carl Hartmann 41
Carl Harmus, Jr...........................42
Adolf Heller................................43

Hard to find mold.

A lovely bisque.

TABLE OF CONTENTS
Questions from Collectors – Answers from an Insider

A little more character...

An endearing expression.

Hertel, Schwab & Co 44

Ernst Heubach 45

Adolf Hülss..................................48

Kämmer & Reinhardt 49

J. D. Kestner, Jr 52

Kley & Hahn 63

Gebrüder Kuhnlenz 65

Limbach Porzellanfabrik 68

Armand Marseille........................69

Porzellanfabrik Mengersgereuth .76

Ernst Metzler 77

Gebrüder Ohlhaver 78

Theodore Recknagel....................79

Bruno Schmidt.............................80

Franz Schmidt & Co....................81

Peter Scherf 82

Schoenau & Hoffmeister.............83

Simon & Halbig...........................86

Schuetzmeister & Quendt............90

Unknown Manufacturers.............91

Tips for Collecting Dolly Faces 94

For Further Reading 85

A Little History

This doll is a 23in (58cm) French child by Emile Jumeau, creator of the child doll, which was quickly adopted and copied by the German doll manufacturers. She is of the type referred to by collectors as an extreme almond-eyed model. *Jim Fernando Collection.*

This outstanding 27-1/2in (70cm) German bisque doll is from the J. D. Kestner firm, known for fine quality dolls and bodies. She is mold number 164. *H & J Foulke, Inc.*

The bisque-head child doll was an invention of the French doll manufacturer Emile Jumeau. In 1878, he won a Gold Medal for his *Bébé* or child doll. Dolls up to this time, whether of French or German manufacture, had been primarily lady dolls with shoulder heads on kid or cloth bodies. But Jumeau claims to have conceived the idea of a child doll. His new *Bébés* had bodies of papier-mâché and wood which were fully jointed and in child proportions. This whole concept of the child doll was quite an innovation and rocked the doll manufacturing world. Not only was the head a revolution, but the body was a whole new fabrication with full maneuverability because it was jointed at neck

6

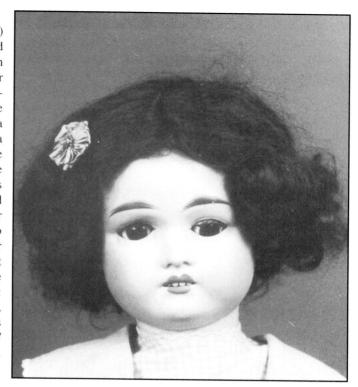

This 24in (61cm) doll is marked only "Made in Germany." Her quality is not outstanding, and she is probably from a Sonneberg area factory, but she has some nice features such as her well-painted eyebrows and her real eyelashes. To collectors her most important aspect is that she is totally original: wig, clothes, underwear, shoes and socks. *H & J Foulke, Inc.*

shoulder, elbows, hips and knees. Within months of Jumeau's introduction, *Bébés* became the rage, and all of the French producers began making the new child dolls. They soon largely displaced the lady dolls. The French achieved their finest results in doll making with the *Bébés*, which were idealized and romanticized portraits of children.

The first Jumeau *Bébé* was the so-called almond-eyed Jumeau. A beautiful example is shown on page 5. The face is definitely related to the Jumeau lady dolls, but with larger eyes and a chubbier visage. It didn't take long for the German doll makers to take note of this new French success. They immediately began producing their own child dolls. Indeed, there is a Jumeau doll in one of the German museums today which is said to have been brought home by one of the German makers. Still, the beautiful

An 18in (46cm) German bisque-head child doll incised only "50" with a "/" and size number; this doll is by an unidentified manufacturer. She has many qualities of the French dolls, including pale bisque, lovely blown glass eyes, dark and heavy eyebrows and a mohair wig. A factor which makes her desirable to dolly-face collectors is her square cut teeth. *H & J Foulke, Inc.*

French dolls became the standard for judging child dolls. French products in general, not only in dolls, had the connotation of being the best quality and the most wonderful in the world.

Competition became quite keen between the French and German doll producers. But the Germans opted for what they could do best: manufacture a large quantity of dolls cheaply.

They left luxury up to the French and fabricated basic bisque-head child dolls. For the next 30 years, German factories were primarily producing copies of French dolls. But, with their vast natural resources – supplies of kaolin and wood – and their virtually unlimited supply of cheap labor, the Germans could develop and sell their dolls at a much lower price than the French could.

Many German dolls were just as fine as the French ones. German porcelain factories such as Simon & Halbig and Kestner & Co. poured top-of-the-line bisque heads. Heinrich Handwerck and Kämmer & Reinhardt made high quality fully jointed composition and wood bodies. Because the French first invented this type of body, it was referred to at the time as "French" jointed, even in cases where bodies were made in Germany. The German factories were noted for innovation, and they developed sleeping eyes with many different kinds of movement, open mouths with inset or molded teeth, voice boxes of various types, real eyelash-

This 25in (64cm) doll from mold 275 illustrates French qualities that the porcelain factory of Bähr & Pröschild is known for: heavy eyebrows and large lustrous eyes. This mold was registered in 1891. *H & J Foulke, Inc.*

es and real eyebrows. They experimented widely with both composition and kid body movement.

In leaving luxury to the French – particularly fantastic clothing and accessories – and concentrating on the basic dolls, the Germans developed a thriving and profitable trade. Indeed, the German doll industry produced a dynasty of interrelated families and generations living in palatial residences. Whole villages relied on the doll industry for a living. Many facets of doll making were carried out as a cottage industry with whole families participating in various aspects of doll production such as making bodies, wigs, shoes and other items. Because German dolls were affordable for the middle classes, dolls became accessible to hundreds of millions of children who could not have purchased French dolls.

The manufacture of bisque-head dolls in Thüringia, in what is now called Germany, was for the most part concentrated in two major areas. In northern Thüringia was the Waltershausen/Ohrdruf area. J. D. Kestner was the first doll manufacturer in the area and

A lovely 28in (71cm) 1349 *Jutta*, from the Dressel factory, showing her attractive face with lovely decorating detail. *H & J Foulke, Inc.*

This close-up view is of Heinrich Handwerck's mold 119 in totally original clothing and outstanding condition. A doll like this brings a premium over "book" price. See page 37 for a full view of her. *H & J Foulke, Inc.*

thus became the founder or "father" of the Waltershausen/Ohrdruf doll industry. Seeing the great success and prosperity of Kestner, other factories opened there. The Ohrdruf area porcelain factories were the first to make bisque heads for dolls. These factories produced the finest grade of bisque, and their heads became known around the world for fine quality. They are respected by collectors today just as they were then.

It should be noted that very few factories made both doll heads and bodies. Most heads were made by porcelain factories that supplied more than one doll factory. Doll factories made the bodies and assembled the dolls, adding wigs and sometimes

This 24in (61cm) girl is from Ernst Heubach's mold 250, a socket head on a jointed composition and wood body. This is a very nice example with multi-stroked eyebrows, large eyes, lip shading and old wig. When buying a more common doll of this type, look for the prettiest, best quality doll that you can find. *H & J Foulke,*

clothing. The following are the porcelain factories that made bisque heads in the Waltershausen/Ohrdruf area and the dates which they were established. Some of these factories were established early enough to have made china head dolls before the bisque ones came into fashion.

Simon & Halbig, 1869

Alt, Beck & Gottschalck, 1854
Kling & Co., 1870
Bähr & Pröschild, 1871
Hertel, Schwab & Co., 1910
Kestner & Co., 1860 (the only one of these factories that made complete dolls)
Schuetzmeister & Quendt, 1889

Just over the mountain and to the south of Waltershausen was the city of Sonneberg, which had a history of doll making going back hundreds of years. However, the manufacture of bisque heads was late coming to this area and did not start until the 1880s. Although eventually millions of doll heads came out of the Sonneberg factories, they did not produce the same fine qual-

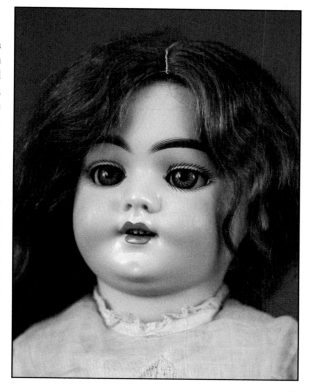

This 18in (46cm) girl is a lovely example from Simon & Halbit's mold 1009, which has almost a smiling expression. Some French producers, including Jumeau and S.F.B.J., used S & H heads, and this is such an example because she is on a French jointed body. It is not rare to find S & H heads on French bodies, and it is a correct combination. The 1009 mold dates from 1889 but was used for quite a few years. It is thought that heads without the word "Germany" were made before 1892. *H & J Foulke, Inc.*

These Armand Marseille dolls incised "Florodora" are interesting because they have their original factory clothes. The styles are not bad, but the fabrics are very cheap and the decoration is placed only on the front. The heads are not as well finished as those on larger A.M. dolls but are typical of the small inexpensive type. However, in spite of quality, any all original doll is very collectible. *H. & J Foulke, Inc.*

ity of bisque as the Ohrdruf manufacturers. Their dolls were economy models at the lower end of the market. And, with few exceptions, that is how they are regarded by today's collectors. The following is a list of the manufacturers of bisque heads in the Sonneberg area.

Theodore Recknagel, 1886

Swain & Co., 1910

Ernst Heubach, 1887

Gebrüder Kuhnlenz,1884

Porzellanfabrik Mengersgereuth, 1908

Limbach, dolls' heads from 1893-1899 and 1919 on

Gebrüder Knoch, 1887

William Goebel, 1879

Schoenau & Hoffmeister, 1901 (also made complete dolls)

Armand Marseille, 1885 (also made complete dolls)

Hermann Steiner, 1909 (also made complete dolls)

Max Oscar Arnold, 1877 (also made complete dolls)

The German bisque doll dominated the doll market, both worldwide and in the United States, from about 1880 until the 1930s. By then, the United States was producing high quality composition dolls which were unbreakable and became the choice of American parents.

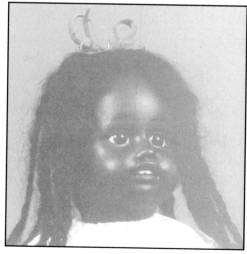

This black bisque doll from the porcelain factory of Gebrüder Kuhnlenz is incised only "34-29." It is certainly a spectacular doll. Little is known about her production, but she is believed to have been made for the French trade. She comes in sizes from 7in (18cm) up. This example is 21in (53cm) tall. *Ruth Covington West.*

THE DOLLY FACE

The German bisque doll which was produced in the largest quantity was the "dolly-face" model. If you are not sure what a dolly-face doll is, just look through the photographs in this book, and you'll see her – for all of the dolls shown have dolly faces. The term simply refers to the basic bisque-head child made from 1880 until 1910. She simply looks at you with a somber visage, maybe a hint of a smile. But she doesn't laugh, cry or pout. These actions were left to the character dolls, which were introduced in 1910 and had faces based on real children. But the character dolls never did surpass the popularity of the "dolly face," which continued to be made in great quantities along with the character dolls.

The earliest bisque dolly faces made by the French had fixed glass eyes and closed mouths. So did those of the Germans, although they were quick to develop and to make widespread use of the weighted glass sleeping eyes. The bisque-head open-mouth doll showing teeth came onto the market in a big way about 1890. Early examples have inserted square cut teeth – sometimes both upper and lower teeth. These square cut teeth are very desirable to collectors. An 1888 advertisement from Kestner & Co. porcelain factory notes bisque doll heads with inserted teeth. This is the earliest date I have found for open-mouth dolls. Other 1888 references are noted in *Ridley's Fashion Magazine*, where an open-mouth doll was priced higher than a comparable one with closed mouth. After all, this open mouth was a new invention. *Youth's Companion* for 1888 described its premium doll for that year: "Its lips are beautifully moulded and slightly parted, showing pearly porcelain teeth which have been naturally inserted." While most dolls had inserted teeth, some, such as

16

Kestner's 154 small dolls and 168 models, had molded-in teeth. The open- and closed-mouth German dolls continued to be made side by side into the 1890s, when the open mouth completely took over and the closed mouth was discontinued.

What Is Bisque?

Bisque is unglazed porcelain. It is translucent. If you hold it up to the light, you can see the light through it. Porcelain is the material used to make your good china dishes. Porcelain is made from a carefully composed mixture of kaolin, fine sand, and the minerals feldspar and quartz. Early manufacturers made a paste of this mix and rolled it out like dough, then pressed it into molds. Later methods used a more liquid slip, which could be poured into molds. (If you look inside a bisque head you can tell whether it was pressed or poured. If it was pressed, the inside will be rough and the thickness uneven. If it was poured, the inside will be smooth and of a uniform thickness.) When the heads are set, the molds are removed, and any openings, such as eyes or mouths, are cut. Then the heads are cleaned and fired at a very high temperature in a large kiln or oven until they become hard. After the heads cool, they are sanded until they are very smooth. Next, they are painted – first with the complexion tint. After that is dry, the heads are ready for the features to be painted: eyebrows, eyelashes, lips, cheeks. After this, the heads are fired again to set the color. This time the result is finished doll heads. The making of bisque heads is a very exacting process involving many complicated steps; at any one of these steps something could go wrong and cause an inferior product.

Bisque as a material for doll heads was actually a German innovation of the 1860s that became very popular, even spreading to France. Doll head materials previous to bisque were wood, papier-mâché, wax and china. Although it was breakable, bisque proved to be the most satisfactory material because of its translucence, which enabled it to have a more natural appearance. Even though other materials were used concurrently, bisque was a popular medium for doll heads and continued to be used widely for 70 years.

The Bodies

Basically there were two types of bisque dolly-face dolls: the shoulder head and the socket head.

The shoulder head was molded with head, neck and shoulders all in one piece. It was mounted on a body of kid or leather. Sometimes, for cheaper dolls, cloth was used. The early kid bodies were sewn together with gusseted joints, which, when they get old and stiff or clogged with the sawdust filler, are not maneuverable. In the 1890s, a rivet-jointed kid body was developed, which allowed for greater movement. For an example see page 62. Dolls with rivet-jointed bodies were more expensive than dolls with gusseted bodies. Quality also came into consideration in the manufacture of the lower arms and lower legs of bisque dolls, some of which were much better finished than others. The better dolls had kid lower legs, and the less expensive dolls had lower legs made of cloth, which was a cheaper material. Some of the cheaper dolls of the 1920s are on imitation kid bodies – something similar to oilcloth. If you are buying a doll, you should examine all of these body points.

Twenty-five years ago when I first became interested in dolls, collectors regarded the German kid-bodied dolls as second class, and some of this prejudice still survives today, but to a lesser extent. It really is a very short-sighted person who rejects a German doll simply because it has a kid body rather than judging the doll on its own merits: its face and its quality. Many of the Simon & Halbig, Kestner and Armand Marseille shoulder heads are excellent quality.

I think part of the reason some collectors regard German shoulder head dolls as inferior lies in the fact that some of the later ones are definitely of lesser quality, particularly the smaller ones on which the painting and decoration are done in an indifferent manner – making a few of them downright ugly. On some, the eyes are carelessly set, causing a cross-eyed appearance, and even the bisque hands are the cheapest possible quality. However, at the time they were made, these dolls filled a need to supply dolls to the masses. It is interesting to note that in 1899 a 10 inch (25 centimeter) doll with bisque shoulder head wholesaled from Butler Brothers for less than eight cents. At those prices no one expected top quality. But I think that, before the whole production of shoulder head dolls is dismissed because of a few, they should be examined individually and judged on their special merits: appealing faces, smoothness of bisque, even face complexion, well-painted eyebrows and eyelashes, pretty lips and eyes with good quality irises. All of these attributes can be found on bisque shoulder head dolls.

It is a general collecting rule today that kid-bodied dolls are less expensive than ball-jointed ones. This can work in the favor of a collector on a budget because a doll with a shoulder head on a kid body will sell for a lot less than a doll with the same face on a jointed body. This is true for many of the Simon & Halbig dolls, as well as for other dolls that came on both types of bodies.

The other type of bisque head is a socket model that goes on a bisque shoulder plate mounted on a kid body or on a jointed wood and composition child body. Bachmann credits Heinrich Stier of Sonneberg with introducing the ball-jointed body to the German doll industry in about 1880. Ball-jointed bodies became popular almost immediately even though they were more expensive than the kid bodies. Consumers then, as collectors now, preferred the way the bodies could assume poses, even sit easily. Examples of German ball-jointed bodies are shown on pages 51, 54 and 70. However, even ball-jointed bodies are of varying quality. The premium companies made very sturdy bodies, using wood for some of the parts and for the joints. The lesser companies frequently used more composition and sometimes even used heavy, shaped cardboard stapled together for torsos and upper limbs. Sometimes on the smaller bisque-head dolls from the Sonneberg area, cheaply made bodies with so-called "stick legs" were used. These are thin, turned wood upper legs, which are not very attractive. For an example, see page 72. Many collectors do not like these bodies, but when dolls are dressed you do not notice them. When buying a doll, always examine the body to check not only condition but quality. You don't expect the body to be perfect, and some repair is fine, but a doll's body should be sturdy and structurally sound.

THE MARKS

Fortunately for doll collectors today, most manufacturers of bisque head dolls put quite a bit of information on the backs of their doll heads. Sometimes you have to loosen the wig and gently pull it up to see the complete mark. Be careful not to tear the cloth wig cap. You can dampen it if it doesn't give easily. Shoulder head dolls are marked across the bottom of the back shoulder plate; some are marked across the front. For these dolls you have to gently pull down the kid. Generally, it will come down easily, because the old glue has dried out over the years; however, be careful not to tear the kid. If it is stubborn, sometimes dampening it can help.

The marks are important because they identify the doll for you by providing such information as the trade name, the maker, the country of origin, the style or mold number, the registration number, or even the patent date. Marks and labels are also important because they give you, as the buyer, confidence that you know exactly what you are buying and can locate it in the **Blue Book of Dolls & Values**® or in a doll encyclopedia.

Also, look on the bodies of the dolls for factory marks. This is especially important for dolls by Heinrich Handwerck and J. D. Kestner, both of whom marked their jointed bodies – Handwerck with his full name and Kestner with a red rectangle stamp. When the body is marked, you know you have the correct head/body combination. You want to avoid buying a K & R head on a Kestner body. Sometimes you will find store stamps or labels on the bodies. Kid bodies often have manufacturers' or distributors' labels or stamps on the front of the torso.

SAMPLE DOLL MARKS

1. Simon & Halbig

2. Bruno Schmidt

3. Gebrüder Kuhnlenz

4. Alt, Beck & Gottschalck (back shoulder)

5. Porzellanfabrik Mengersgereuth

6. Simon & Halbig for Kämmer & Reinhardt

7. Gebrüder Kuhnlenz

8. Cuno & Otto Dressel

9. Armand Marseille

10. Simon & Halbig

11. Alt, Beck & Gottschalck (after 1910)

12. Armand Marseille

13. J. D. Kestner

14. Armand Marseille

15. J. D. Kestner

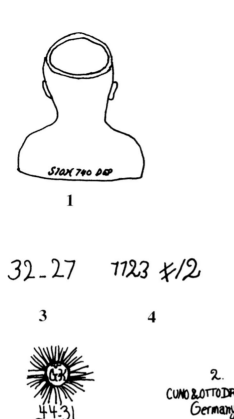

1

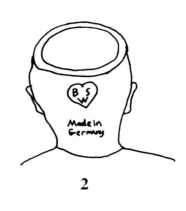

2

32-27

3

7123 ✗/2

4

Trebor
Germany
P.O.M.

5

SIMON & HALBIG
K ✡ R
5.5.

6

44-31
Dep.

7

2.
CUNO & OTTO DRESSEL.
Germany.

8½

8

1894
AM8DEP

9

SH1039
10½DEP

10

AR
1362
Made in Germany
2¼
9½

11

29
Queen Louise
Germany
7½.

12

B made in 6
Germany
143.

13

2015 ⚓ 4/0

14

Made in Germany
C½.168. 7½

15

THE DOLLS

Alt, Beck & Gottschalck

The Alt, Beck & Gottschalck porcelain factory was located in Nauendorf, Thüringia, Germany, near Ohrdruf, home of the better known Kestner & Co. Years ago, many collectors attributed heads that we now know were made by ABG to Kestner. It is not surprising that two factories located so close together would have a similar style because it is likely that workers went back and forth between the two companies as needed. The finest quality German doll heads came from this Waltershausen/Ohrdruf area

This lovely ABG girl is a turned shoulder head model from mold 1235. A "turned" head is molded with a stiff neck but, instead of looking straight out, the head is turned slightly - usually to the right. She has slightly parted lips with teeth. Usually ABG used the designation "1/2" after the mold number of dolls with open mouths. The letters "dep," meaning registered or copyrighted, were added after 1888. Not only does she have the beautiful creamy bisque known to be produced by the ABG factory, she came to us in completely original condition, including blonde mohair wig and clothes. She should be considered a choice example of her type. *H & J Foulke, Inc.*

of northern Thüringia. The ABG factory was in operation as early as 1854. Their early heads are china and bisque shoulder models with molded hair. Before 1910, ABG marked the back edge of their shoulder plates with a mold number and the marks: ⋈, ⋈ , or N0. ABG was an important participant in the marking of doll heads, with a large export of heads to the United States as early as 1882. The ABG factory made china and bisque heads and parts only. They did not make bodies or complete dolls. At one time, the company had 300 factory workers and 100 families working at home.

This 22in (56cm) girl from mold 1362 was marketed as *Sweet Nell*. She is popular not only because of her pert face but also because of her name. Collectors seem to like dolls with names. She is a later doll, after 1910 and probably closer to 1920. Dolly faces designed during this period, after the introduction of the character doll in 1910, often have a hint of a character look like *Sweet Nell* has. She has real upper eyelashes (many were made from silk) and lower lashes painted in short, straight lines. She has a socket head on a jointed composition body. ABG heads of this period are often not as fine a quality as the earlier shoulder head dolls. *H & J Foulke, Inc.*

Bähr & Pröschild

The Bähr & Pröschild porcelain factory was established in 1871 in Ohrdruf, Thüringia, Germany. Early products of the factory were china doll heads and bathing children (Frozen Charlottes). The Ohrdruf area was known for fine quality porcelain and excellent craftsmanship. Dolls before 1910 are marked only with a series of 200 and 300 mold numbers, usually accompanied by "dep" in lower case letters to indicate design patent registration. Because there is no company trademark on the doll's head, these dolls have been largely unidentified by the majority of collectors.

Most B & P heads are the socket type mounted on jointed wood and composition bodies. The upper arms and legs are gen-

This small doll is from mold 281. This mold was registered in 1892. Many B.P. dolls of this size are found wearing European regional costumes. Note her pierced ears, another French quality. *H & J Foulke, Inc.*

This sweet 13in (33cm) girl is from mold 297 which was registered in 1893. Her old mohair wig is a replacement dating from the 1920s, from a large group of old factory stock which was recently found in Germany. *H & J Foulke, Inc.*

erally from turned wood, and the lower limbs are composition, often with straight wrists. However, sometimes the lower arms are of wood also, with jointed wrists and separate hands. Body styles will vary, though, because B.P. was a porcelain factory and did not make complete dolls, only the bisque heads. Because of the lovely quality of the bisque, the beautiful inset glass eyes, the heavy eyebrows and the style of the body, many collectors had previously thought that these heads were French.

Mold 224 is one of the most desirable and sought after of the B.P. dollies with open mouths. A distinctive look always makes a doll more valuable. The 224 is characterized by her deep cheek dimples. She is wearing an antique red coat and hat. This choice example is 22in (56cm) tall. B & P registered this number in 1888. This open-mouthed doll is probably from 1890. *H & J Foulke, Inc.*

Mold 360, dating from about 1896, is quite distinctive because of her long cheek line. When buying German dollies, always look for a face that's a little different. She is a large 29in (74cm) tall. *H & J Foulke, Inc.*

This mold 513 is a later doll, which I believe is from the B.P. factory; there is no documentation for her. You can tell that she is later because she has no painted upper eyelashes. Real eyelashes were not widely used until after 1910. This doll has a very desirable old human hair wig with long curls. *H & J Foulke, Inc.*

C.M. Bergmann

The Bergmann doll factory was located in Waltershausen, a thriving Thüringian doll manufacturing area. Bergmann bought bisque heads from porcelain manufacturers, such as Simon & Halbig, Armand Marseille, Alt, Beck & Gottschalck and perhaps others. The factory was founded in 1888, and production was primarily of dolly-faced dolls and some character babies. As a rule of thumb, the A.M. heads, which seem to include mold 1916, are not as attractive and appealing as the heads made by Simon & Halbig, so they do not bring as high a price. When buying Bergmanns, look for a doll with a pretty face. Bergmann made good quality composition and wood jointed bodies.

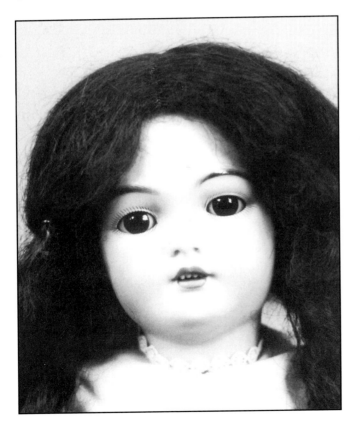

A sweet 22in (56cm) girl incised with the Bergmann name and the Simon & Halbig initials. She has a very appealing face with pretty bisque, dark attractive eyes and old dark brown human hair wig.
H & J Foulke, Inc.

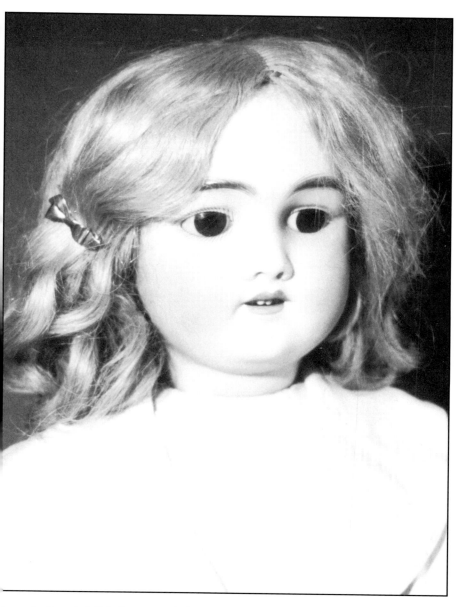

A rarely found doll is Bergmann's incised *Eleonore*, also marked with the Simon & Halbig initials. She is especially desirable to collectors who like dolls with names. The few·times I've seen this doll, she has always been 25in (64cm) tall. Her long glossy eyebrows are heavily molded, indicating a later date than if she had flat eyebrows. *H & J Foulke, Inc.*

Cuno & Otto Dressel

The Dressel firm of Sonneberg was the oldest and largest maker, assembler and distributor of dolls in Germany, having been established in 1700. The Dressels produced a large quantity of goods in their vast factories, but they also bought the complete production of many smaller factories and employed a great number of home workers as well. The Dressels did not have their own factory for the manufacture of porcelain heads. Bisque heads were purchased from Armand Marseille, Ernst Heubach, Schoenau & Hoffmeister, Gebrüder Heubach and Simon & Halbig. Some Dressel composition bodies are stamped on the back of the torso with the winged Dressel trademark.

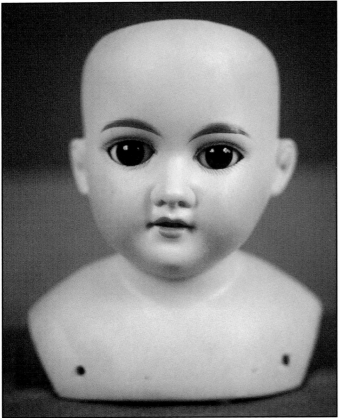

This shoulder head incised "COD 93 AM" was made for Dressel by the Armand Marseille porcelain factory. It is a fine quality bisque with lovely decoration, expressive eyes and appealing face. It dates from 1893, an early production from the A.M. factory made during the time when their finest bisque heads were manufactured. This is a very desirable shoulder head doll for a collector to buy. *H & J Foulke, Inc.*

This 22in (56cm) Dressel doll is mold 1912, which is probably the date of the mold. This probably is also an A.M. head, but it lacks the quality and appeal of the 1893 model. The face is much more ordinary. Attractive hair and clothes do a lot to increase the appeal of this type of doll. *H & J Foulke, Inc.*

An outstanding girl incised only "Cuno & Otto Dressel" with no mold number. She is probably a Simon & Halbig product because she looks very similar to the Kämmer & Reinhardt 117n, which S & H also made. Her quality is excellent, and she is on a very good quality jointed composition body with a high knee joint. Her mohair wig is original. She would date from about 1910. It is hard to know whether to classify a doll such as this as a character doll or dolly-face doll. Certainly the influence of the character doll is noticeable. According to the doll's current owner, this doll was sold as *Big Sister* by the chain of Eaton's Department Stores in Canada. *H & J Foulke, Inc.*

This doll represents the prize of every doll collector — a totally original doll which came to us in her original box. She is Dressel's mold 1349 *Jutta* made for them by Simon & Halbig. This was apparently Dressel's luxury line, as Dressel chose the prestigious firm of S & H to pour the heads, and they are on excellent quality jointed composition bodies, usually with the Dressel trademark on back. The face is very appealing and popular with collectors. The *Jutta* trademark was used from 1906-1921. This example appears to be from about 1920 because of her molded eyebrows and real eyelashes. Other quality features are her human hair wig and pink leather shoes. *H & J Foulke, Inc.*

Heinrich Handwerck

Heinrich Handwerck, located in Waltershausen, operated a well-respected firm in the doll industry, having started business in 1855. Not having a porcelain factory, Handwerck engaged Simon & Halbig to pour heads for him after his own designs. Fortunately for doll collectors today, all of Handwerck's heads are fully and clearly marked. His face designs are very attractive and are sought after by today's collectors. The Handwerck bodies are sturdy composition and wood models, stamped in black or red with the Handwerck name. Always look for the stamp when buying a Handwerck doll to be sure it is on the correct body.

A very pretty Handwerck girl from mold 69, this doll has quite a full face; her deep set, almond-shaped eyes are quite unusual. Always look for an unusual feature when buying a dolly-faced doll. *H & J Foulke, Inc.*

This sweet 15in (38cm) doll is incised with the Handwerck and S & H trademarks with no mold number. Some of the faces with no mold number are not as attractive as the numbered faces, but this one is very sweet. She has molded eyebrows and still retains her upper eyelashes. *H & J Foulke, Inc.*

This large 25in (64cm) Handwerck is from seldom-found mold 199. She has a lovely, wistful expression on her face. Her French long curl human hair wig is a good quality replacement. Recently, excellent large size mohair wigs have become available from German, French and U.S. companies and this type would also be appropriate for her. When replacing wigs, avoid shiny synthetic ones that do not have a natural look. *H & J Foulke, Inc.*

A totally original doll from Handwerck's mold 119, this doll is truly a rarity in her factory or store clothing. Most dolls from this period were sold wearing only a chemise and sometimes shoes and socks. Dolls dressed like this one in quality clothing were expensive and were available only in better department stores or exclusive toy stores. She is 19in (48cm) tall. *H & J Foulke, Inc.*

Max Handwerck

The Max Handwerck doll factory was also located in Waltershausen, but it generally does not have the reputation that the Heinrich Handwerck factory has. Some of Max Handwerck's *Bébé Elite* trademark heads were made by Goebel, but most M. Handwerck heads have not been attributed to a porcelain factory. Max was late entering the doll business, only starting production in 1900. His dolls are socket heads on good, but not the best quality, jointed composition bodies.

A typical Max Handwerck girl incised with his trademark signature. These heads are of singular design in that they have an extremely high forehead and look rather peculiar when they have no wig on. She is 25in (64cm) tall. *H & J Foulke, Inc.*

This Max Handwerck from mold 421 is one of his better faces with a much more appealing look. The bisque is also a better quality, but the porcelain factory is unknown, although it looks like bisque from the Waltershausen/Ohrdruf area. It must have been his top-of-the-line model. Some of these 421 dolls are incised "M.Handwerck" and some only "Handwerck," and I have had one with the body stamped in red "Max Handwerck," so there is no doubt about the maker. This is a lovely doll worth searching for. *H & J Foulke, Inc.*

Karl Hartmann

Karl Hartmann was another late entrant into the doll industry, starting in 1911. He made a good quality doll but not an outstanding one, although sometimes a doll turns up with an extremely pretty face, such as that shown in the **11th Blue Book** on page 194. The Hartmann mark is a large "H" with curved sides and a small "K" above the cross bar.

This 19in (48cm) girl has the typical Karl Hartmann look. She has real upper eyelashes and no painted upper lashes. She is totally original in store or factory clothes with organdy and lace trimmed dress with buttons and buttonholes on the back, lots of white cotton underwear and blue cloth shoes. Any old dolls in original clothes are very desirable. *H & J Foulke, Inc.*

Carl Hartmann

Carl Hartmann founded his factory in 1889. He was a maker and exporter of dressed dolls. Although Hartmann sold a wide variety of dolls, the only ones I have been able to locate that I know are by him are his trademarked *Globe Babies*. These are not actually babies but are child dolls.

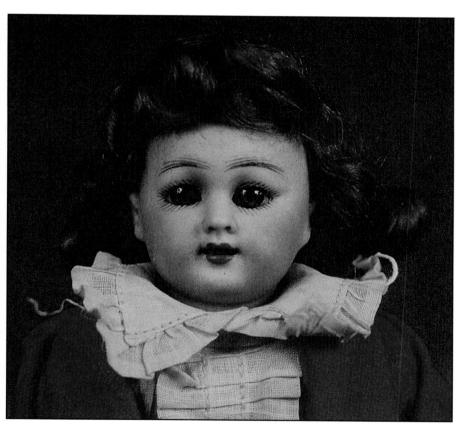

This 8in (20cm) child has the *Globe Baby* trademark incised on the back of his head. It was registered in 1898. All of the *Globe Baby* dolls that I have seen have been this small size. The heads are very good Simon & Halbig quality bisque, but no porcelain factory mark is given; bodies are mediocre quality. It is very desirable to find *Globe Babies* in original good quality clothes. *H & J Foulke, Inc.*

Carl Harmus, Jr.

Carl Harmus had a doll factory in Sonneberg starting in 1887. He also exported dolls. Few dolls have been found with his mark. Probably, like so many of the smaller doll factories, instead of having heads made especially for him with his own mark, he used stock heads that could be supplied by any of the porcelain factories. These he put on his own bodies or bodies that he purchased from another doll factory. The heads would carry the porcelain factory mark instead of the doll factory mark. Examples of stock heads include Simon & Halbig's 1079 model. S & H sold this head to numerous doll factories. Unless the bodies were marked, it would be impossible to know the doll factory responsible for the complete doll.

Incised with the Harmus name, there is no doubt that this 20in (51cm) girl is from his factory. She has a very appealing face and appears to be from the 1920s. She has no painted upper eyelashes, so originally would have had real ones. As often happens, the eyelashes disintegrated or were eaten away by insects. The fact that they are missing does not devalue the doll. Actually, real original eyelashes are a plus factor in evaluating a doll. This girl has a very pretty original wig, which matches her eyebrows. *H & J Foulke, Inc.*

Adolf Heller

This is another small doll factory in Waltershausen, which operated from 1909-1930. Like Harmus, little is found with Heller's mark, probably for the same reasons.

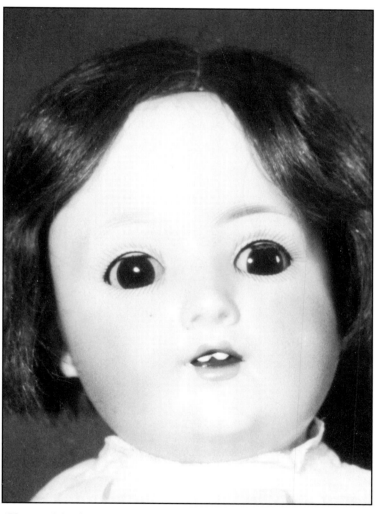

A 21in (53cm) girl with the incised "A.H." mark of Heller. She is good quality bisque with multi-stroked eyebrows and nice face tinting. Her two upper teeth give her a distinctive look, although she may at one time have had the traditional four teeth. She is on a 1920s flapper body with high knee joint so that she can wear above-the-knee dresses without showing an ugly ball-joint. She is very rarely found. *H & J Foulke, Inc.*

Hertel, Schwab & Co.

Hertel, Schwab & Co. was an important porcelain factory near Ohrdruf founded in 1910 by two sculptors. As such, it is no wonder that their main production was character dolls and babies. For years, the products of this company were attributed to Kestner because the existence of H.S. & Co. was unknown. It is not surprising that their heads are so like Kestner's since the factories are located very close together. The two companies probably even had some of the same decorators working for them. The Hertel, Schwab bisque heads are of very fine quality and very desirable to collectors. Among doll factories familiar to collectors, H.S. & Co. made heads for Koenig & Wernicke; Kley & Hahn; Wiesenthal, Schindel & Kallenberg; George Borgfeldt & Co.; Louis Wolf & Co.; and Strobel & Wilken.

This 24-1/2in (62cm) girl is incised with the mold number "136." Hertel, Schwab dolls do not carry a porcelain factory trademark. They are marked only with a mold number or with a mold number and trademark of the doll factory producing the doll. The 136 girl is very desirable. This is the only dolly-face mold that I am aware of from the Hertel, Schwab factory.

This example from the 1920s has almost a character look to her face. She wears her original mohair wig and what may be an original homemade outfit. *H & J Foulke, Inc.*

44

Ernst Heubach

Ernst Heubach established a porcelain factory in Köppelsdorf, near Sonneberg, in 1887. He produced many mediocre quality small heads, but also a surprising number of very nicely decorated heads. Some of his character baby models are very appealing. From 1919 until 1932, the Ernst Heubach porcelain factory was united with that of Armand Marseille through the marriage of their children. Heubach's shoulder head dolls of the early 1900s can be identified by his horseshoe trademark.

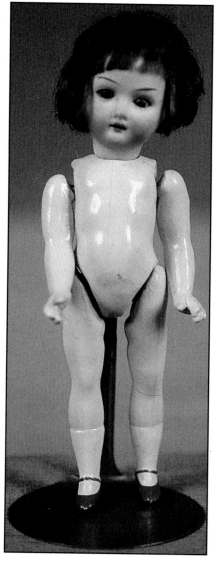

A 7-1/2in (19cm) mold 250 girl of the 1920s. Because of her short bobbed mohair wig and slender arms and legs, she is called by collectors a flapper doll. Her body is good quality composition with molded and painted shoes and stockings. When buying these small dolls, always look for examples with extra nice painting and good quality, shapely bodies. Some small heads of inexpensive dolls were put on very crude bodies that seem to be made only of sawdust and cardboard. I would avoid these unless they happened to have original clothes. Then they can become quite interesting. *H & J Foulke, Inc.*

This 15in (38cm) Ernst Heubach child is from shoulder head mold 275 on a kid body with bisque lower arms. Her bisque and decoration are not great, but a plus factor is her original factory or store outfit which is of quite nice quality, with fabric that is not as flimsy as is generally found on these inexpensive dolls. She also has her original wig. On inexpensive dolls, the wigs are not sewn and are often just hanks of mohair glued onto a wig cap or pushed through a hole in a cardboard pate. A totally original doll is always an important addition to a collection. *H & J Foulke, Inc.*

This interesting 24in (61cm) flapper doll with high knee joint was made by E.H. for the Seyfarth & Reinhardt doll factory and is incised with mold number "312" and their "SuR" trademark, which they registered in 1923. She has good bisque and the very rosy cheek color which came into vogue for dolls in the 1920s. Her hair is original. She would be a nice addition to a collection of flapper dolls because she is not an easy doll to find. *H & J Foulke, Inc.*

Adolf Hülss

Adolf Hülss opened his doll factory in 1913. He specialized in character babies but also had some child dolls. He had heads made by Simon & Halbig after his own designs and carrying the Hülss trademark – the letters "AHW" in a circle. Hülss dolls are excellent quality and very desirable. Hülss sold not only complete dolls but also separate heads, body parts and wigs.

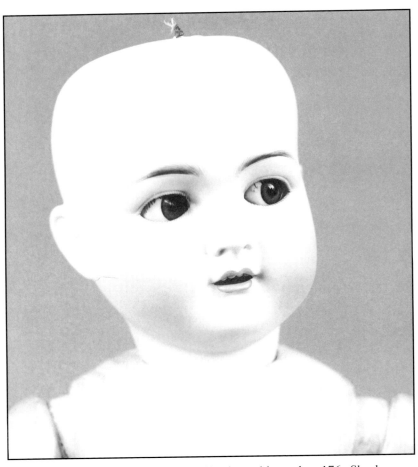

Seldom is the Hülss dolly face found. She is mold number 176. She has a very expressive face and could almost be called a character doll. Her eyes are flirty, which means that they move from side to side when her head is tilted. Her jointed composition body has a high knee joint. She is a very desirable doll of the 1920s. *H & J Foulke, Inc.*

Kämmer & Reinhardt

The Kämmer & Reinhardt doll factory of Waltershausen is without a doubt one of the most respected makers of German bisque dolls. The factory began in 1886, but their most famous products were not made until after the 1910 introduction of the character doll. Most of the K & R heads were poured by the prestigious Simon & Halbig porcelain factory after K & R's own designs. K & R dolls are of excellent quality, including their composition and wood jointed bodies. After 1895, they are marked with their famous "K ★ R" trademark.

This early K & R model is from mold 192 and dates from 1892. It is not known who made these early bisque heads, but they have many characteristics which suggest the Kestner porcelain factory. The 192 mold is very desirable to collectors. This example has a lovely, creamy complexion, beautifully painted dark eyebrows, pronounced philtrum and pretty shading on her slightly parted lips. She has an old blonde mohair wig, which is very desirable on these early dolls. It is much better for a doll to have a nice old wig like this one, even if it is a little scraggly, than a new one. *H & J Foulke, Inc.*

This 19in (48cm) K & R, mold number 403, is lovely bisque with a very nice face. She has a composition and wood walking body with shapely legs, and a head that moves from side to side. She has an old mohair wig and clothing from the 1920s. *H & J Foulke, Inc.*

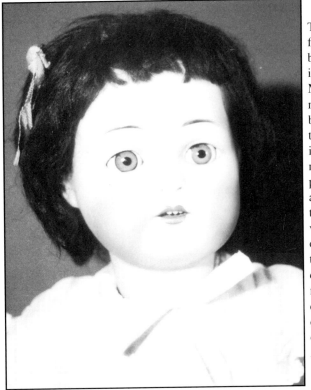

This 22in (56cm) K & R flapper has no mold number, only a size number incised low on her neck. Many collectors do not realize that the size number is her height in centimeters. She is 56cm and is incised "56." That is not a mold number, simply her size. Hundreds and hundreds of people think they have found very rare mold numbers on K & R dolls when all they have found are dolls' sizes. This is the most frequently asked question I receive. This doll is a lovely example of her type. *H & J Foulke, Inc.*

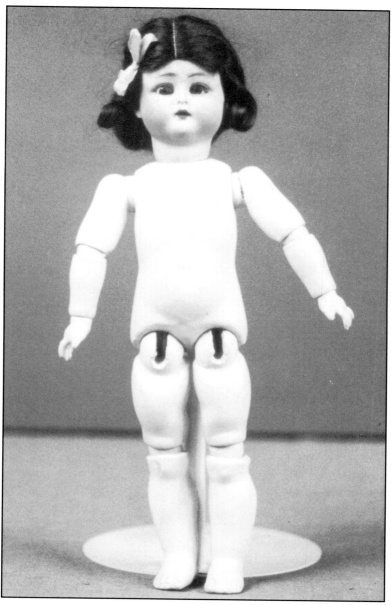

This 13-1/2in (34cm) K & R child is showing her body because, when buying K & R dolls, it is important to be sure the doll is on a K & R body. They are not marked but, with a little study, it is fairly easy to recognize K & R bodies. The torso, hands, upper legs and lower legs are composition; the upper and lower arms are wood. Some K & R bodies have rubber hands. Earlier bodies are yellowish - later ones more pink. This doll's centimeter size on the back of her neck is "34." *H & J Foulke, Inc.*

J. D. Kestner, Jr.

J. D. Kestner, Jr., is the most important name in the history of German doll production in the Waltershausen area, since he was the pioneer founder of the doll industry there, starting in 1816. In 1860, he purchased a porcelain factory in Ohrdruf. This was important because it made him the only German doll producer to make both heads and bodies – hence a complete doll. Later, Armand Marseille (after 1890) and Schoenau & Hoffmeister (after 1901) both made complete dolls. Both the heads and bod-

As is characteristic of early Kestner heads, this dolly has no mold number. She has slightly parted lips with the desirable feature of square cut upper teeth. Collectors interpret the square cut teeth as an early feature. She is 12in (31cm) tall with a nice old blonde mohair wig, a type frequently found on Kestner dolls. Her dark eyebrows are typical of Kestner also, as are the pronounced peaks on her upper lip. *H & J Foulke, Inc.*

This 19in (48cm) Kestner 129 is the first of the open-mouth number series and is not an easy number to find. Her lovely, creamy bisque is emphasized by her dramatic dark blue eyes and dark brown eyebrows. She wears her original blonde mohair wig. *H & J Foulke, Inc.*

ies of the Kestner dolls are excellent quality, except for a few small inexpensive dolls. During their production period, the Kestner firm enjoyed a worldwide reputation for fine dolls. Collectors today still respect Kestner dolls. The Kestner mold number and alphabet/number size system which features marks that are easily recognizable on the backs of the dolls' heads or the bottom of the back shoulder plates, was registered in 1897.

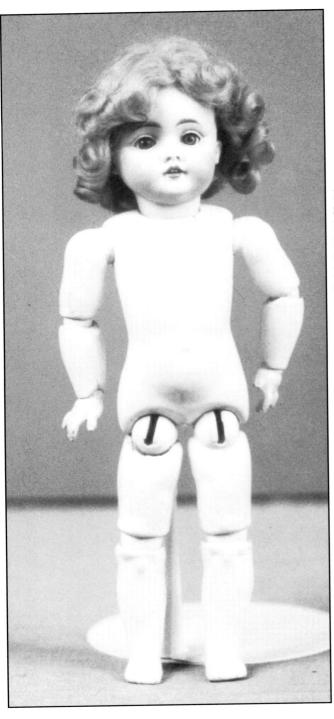

LEFT AND OPPO-SITE PAGE: When buying Kestner dolls, it is important to be sure that they are on Kestner bodies. This doll from mold 143 is on the correct body. Always check the derrière for the red rectangular stamp that Kestner used. Either the trademark "Excelsior" or "Germany" will be inside the red rectangle. Kestner bodies are a combination of sturdy wood and composition. Bodies are usually yellow-ish, but many after 1910 are pinkish. *H & J Foulke, Inc.*

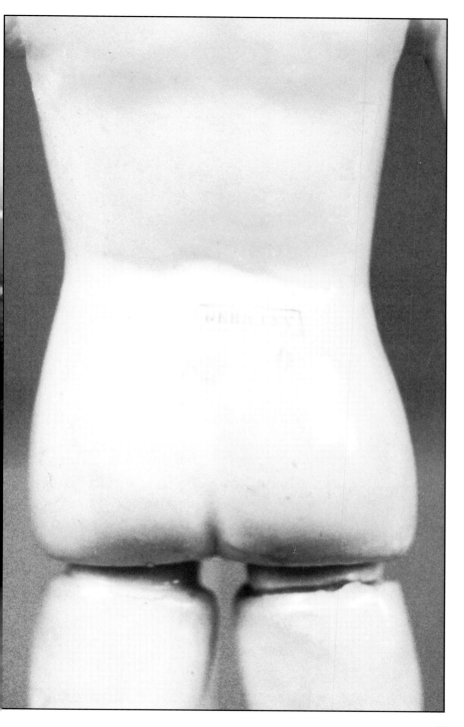

This 24in (61cm) doll is a large and outstanding example of mold 143, a particula favorite of Kestner collectors. Although it has a character-type face, it precedes the introduction of the character doll by about 15 years. I think the 143 mold was intend ed to be a baby doll, in the days long before the baby doll as we think of it was devel oped. The face is quite round for a Kestner doll and has only two upper teeth. I have owned and seen quite a few 143s in their original baby clothes, sometimes very elab orate store outfits. Even though these dolls are dressed in baby clothes, they are on jointed composition child bodies, as the bent-limb baby body had not yet been devel oped. *H & J Foulke, Inc.*

This large 30in (76cm) girl is from mold 164, a favorite with Kestner collectors because the doll is so expressive with her dramatic eyes and eyebrows. A Kestner doll this size is quite substantial because of the heavy, chunky body. *H & J Foulke, Inc.*

This 17in (43cm) Kestner 168 girl has a wistful expression. She is lovely with her original mohair wig and old cotton dress – even a necklace. *H & J Foulke, Inc.*

OPPOSITE PAGE: This 10in (25cm) example of mold 155 is very appealing. She is on a chubby 5-piece, excellent quality composition body with molded and painted shoes and socks. Kestner did not make a large number of dolls that were 10in (25 cm) and under as did Simon & Halbig. This mold is fairly hard to find and always comes in a small size, sometimes on a body with bare feet and jointed knees. *H & J Foulke, Inc.*

This interesting 21in (53cm) Kestner girl incised "J" with turned shoulder head i
part of Kestner's alphabet series. She has lovely bisque and a long, narrow face. She
is on a kid body with bisque lower arms and kid over wood upper arms. She is al
original, including her wig. All original dolls are always a plus factor. *H & J Foulke
Inc.*

OPPOSITE PAGE: This large Kestner 154 is totally original. She is a shoulde
head on a kid body with excellent quality bisque. Obviously she was a luxury doll
as evidenced by her gorgeous satin and lace dress and hat. *H & J Foulke, Inc.*

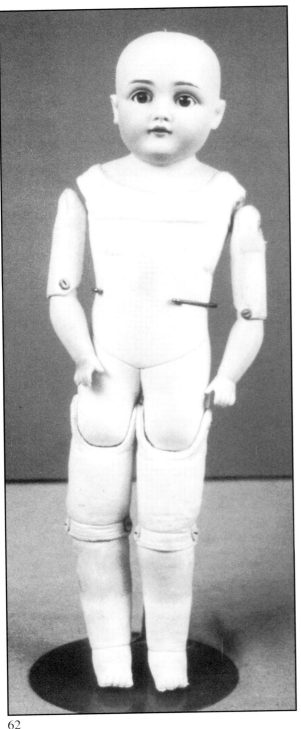

A small Kestner 154 shown to illustrate a typical German kid body. Actually, this is a better quality than most because of the kid over wood upper arms, pin-jointed elbows and lovely bisque lower arms. The rivet joints at hips and knees and the kid lower legs also indicate a quality body. Earlier German bodies have gusseted joints, which get clogged when the sawdust stuffing settles, and are difficult to move. Even after the rivet-jointed kid body was developed, the gusseted one was used for cheaper dolls. Cheaper dolls also had sawdust stuffed kid upper arms and short lower arms which were simply glued on, as well as cloth lower legs and feet. *H & J Foulke, Inc.*

Kley & Hahn

The Kley & Hahn doll factory was established in Ohrdruf in 1895. By this date, the Waltershausen/Ohrdruf area was a well-known doll making center. J.D. Kestner had pioneered the doll industry in this area. Kley & Hahn did not make their own heads, but purchased from Bähr & Pröschild, Hertel, Schwab & Co., and J. D. Kestner. The Kley & Hahn dolls are completely fine quality, both heads and bodies.

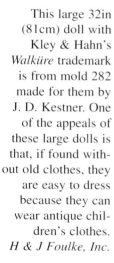

This large 32in (81cm) doll with Kley & Hahn's *Walküre* trademark is from mold 282 made for them by J. D. Kestner. One of the appeals of these large dolls is that, if found without old clothes, they are easy to dress because they can wear antique children's clothes. *H & J Foulke, Inc.*

18-1/2in (47cm) K & H dolly with their *Walküre* trademark, which was registered in 1902. Some of the *Walküre* heads are from mold number 250, which was poured for them by Kestner & Co. This example has a pleasant, pert face. I think these dolls are currently underrated by collectors; there does not seem to be a lot of interest in them, yet they are high quality, attractive dolls. *H & J Foulke, Inc.*

Gebrüder Kuhnlenz

The porcelain factory of Gebrüder Kuhnlenz was located in Kronach, Bavaria. It was founded by three brothers in 1884 and operated until 1935. Their specialty was doll heads. It is only recently that many Kuhnlenz doll heads have been identified

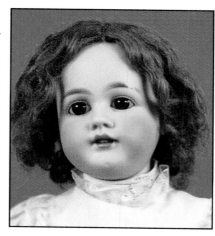

ABOVE: This is a beautiful 24in (61cm) example of G.K.'s mold 44. She has almost a French look to her, with lovely eyes and eyebrows. Kuhnlenz dolls are usually found on early style composition bodies with turned wood upper limbs, but this is not a hard and fast rule since Kuhnlenz sold heads to various doll factories that used their own bodies. *H & J Foulke, Inc.*

RIGHT: This 15in (38cm) example of mold 44 does not have as beautiful a face as the larger mold 44 doll. These photographs are examples of variation in two dolls of the same mold from the same company. When buying dolly faces, always choose the best quality, most expressive example that you can find. This doll is cute but lacks the appeal of the larger one. She is incised "44-23." *H & J Foulke, Inc.*

because many do not carry the trademark, which is "GbrK" or just "GK" in a radiant circle. However, the molding and size system helps identify dolls that do not have the trademark. A two-digit mold number is followed by a dash and a two-digit size number – for instance, "44-23."

No porcelain factory is entirely consistent with markings, and G.K. is no exception. This doll is from mold 165, the only three-digit number found with a Kuhnlenz trademark. She is a much more typical German dolly face than those with the two-digit numbers and probably represents a later period of production – partly evidenced by her molded eyebrows. *H & J Foulke, Inc.*

OPPOSITE PAGE: G.K. produced a lot of small heads from mold 44. They are usually on medium quailty bodies; many still retain their original clothes. This small face is popular because it has somewhat of a character look with its upper square teeth. She is 7in (18cm) tall and is incised "44-17." *H & J Foulke, Inc.*

Limbach Porzellanfabrik

Limbach porcelain factory was founded in 1772. For the most part, they did small figurines, bathing dolls, all-bisques and knick knacks. Among doll collectors they are known mostly for their all-bisque children and babies incised with their cloverleaf trademark. However, they did make doll heads.

This 22in (56cm) girl is incised with the Limbach cloverleaf trademark. Her bisque is a fairly good quality, and her face is pleasant. Limbach bisque heads are not easy to find. The quality varies; some are very pretty, some quite ordinary. This particular model was made during the 1893-1899 period. Doll head production was then discontinued until 1919, when heads bearing the names *Wally, Rita* and *Norma* were introduced. *H & J Foulke, Inc.*

Armand Marseille

Probably the first bisque doll that most people see is one produced by the prolific factory of Armand Marseille in Köppelsdorf, near Sonneberg, Thüringia, Germany. The Marseille factories were the largest manufacturers of doll heads in the world from 1900 until the 1930s. Since he owned both a doll factory and a porcelain factory, Armand Marseille was one of the few German producers who made complete dolls. He also sold bisque heads and bisque parts to a large number of doll factories and jobbers or assemblers for use on their own bodies. Some purchased standard Armand Marseille models, but some had special heads made from their own molds and trademarks.

The loveliest of the A.M. child dolls were made during the first years of the factory in the first half of the 1890s. The first ones were shoulder heads to be used on kid or cloth bodies with bisque lower arms. The mold numbers for this series start with number 1890, which doll researchers have discovered also represents the year the mold was first introduced. For a lovely example of a head in this series, see the Cuno & Otto Dressel section.

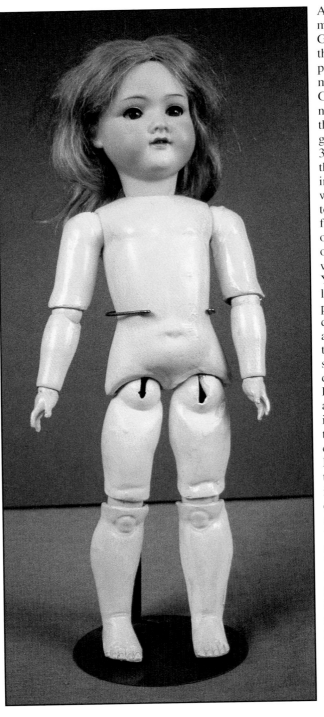

Although the 390 is the most commonly found German bisque "dolly," there are some very pretty examples of this model in existence. Generally the bisque is not as fine as that on the 1894, but it is good. Many of the 390s have lovely, threaded eyes, lip shading and pretty mohair wigs. If adding a 390 to your collection, look for one that is totally original, with factory or store clothes, underwear, shoes and socks. You should always look for the best example you can find of any doll that you are adding to your collection, but sometimes we settle for less when a doll is hard to find. However, with a doll as common as the 390, it is even more important to find the best original example. Many collectors feel that they want to include a 390 in their collections because it is such a typical German "dolly" and is so representative of the genre. This 19in (48cm) 390 is shown to illustrate a typical medium quality German composition and wood body. This particular body is better than one that is made from shaped and stapled cardboard.
H & J Foulke, Inc.

Most collectors would agree that the 1894 face mold is the most beautiful "dolly" that Marseille produced. All of the other 1890s mold numbers came only as shoulder head models, but the 1894 came both as a shoulder head and as a socket head for use on a composition body. However, in looking at dolls from this mold, it must be remembered that it was used for a long period of time - over 30 years - and there is a big difference in quality between the early and later models. The early 1894 socket head is very French in appearance, with dark, heavily stroked eyebrows and stationary, paperweight-type eyes; the bisque is pale and very fine, the lips have accents stroked on the top and bottom. The heads are simply marked "1894//A M [size #] DEP." Some of the later examples and smaller heads are not as nicely decorated. The bodies on the early 1894 socket heads are composition and wood. The torso, lower legs and lower arms with unjointed wrists are of composition; the upper arms and legs are of wood. The early 1894 model deserves an honored place in a collection of German children. This example is 23in (58cm) tall and still retains her beautiful old blonde mohair wig. *H & J Foulke, Inc.*

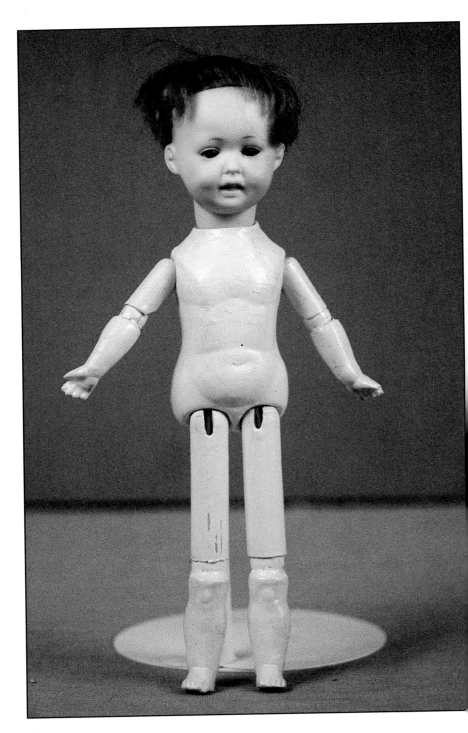

This 24in (61cm) doll is another example of the lovely quality bisque that the A.M. factory could produce. She is from the early 1890s but has no mold number. *H & J Foulke, Inc.*

OPPOSITE PAGE: This photograph illustrates a type of body used by Armand Marseille as well as other German makers of inexpensive dolls. These were generally used on dolls under 16in (41cm). Collectors refer to these as bodies with "stick legs." They are certainly not very attractive, but they are authentic. If you have a choice, look for a doll on a better quality body, but, if the doll is all original and you like it, you will have to settle for its body. The head on this body is an A.M. 590 character boy. *H & J Foulke, Inc.*

A.M. made a large number of sho[ul]der head dolls. Generally dolls w[ith] shoulder heads and kid or cloth b[od]ies are the "step children" of [a] German doll collection. They [are] not particularly popular with coll[ec]tors because they are not as flexi[ble] as the composition bodied do[lls] and they are not as easy to po[se.] Also, the bodies sometimes [get] wear spots and leak sawdust. [Of] course, this keeps the price lo[wer] than for comparable composit[ion] body dolls, so, these dolls are app[re]ciated by the thrifty collec[tor.] Marseille's most often found sho[ul]der head is mold 370. The shoul[der] head doll in this photograph, ho[w]ever, is from mold 2015, which [is] not as commonly found. She is [14] 1/2in (37cm) tall. *H & J Fou[nd] Inc.*

Baby Betty is a popular A[.M.] doll because she has [an] unusual face with a sw[eet] smiling expression. Her na[me] is incised in her bisque. [She] comes as both a shoul[der] head and a socket head, m[ade] for Butler Brothers in 19[.] The quality of the bisque [and] decoration of the head is u[su]ally very good. *H & J Fou[nd] Inc.*

Queen Louise is another popular A.M. name doll. Although she is not rare, collectors really like her. I remember that the first bisque doll I ever looked at was a *Queen Louise*. I thought then that she was pretty, and I still think so. She was made by A.M. for Louis Wolfe & Co. in 1910 and in the following years. Because this is an available doll, if you buy one, look for an example with a very pretty face and a body in excellent condition. *H & J Foulke, Inc.*

A.M. made a lot of small inexpensive dolls with bisque heads, the smallest I'm aware of is 4-1/2in (12 cm) tall. The composition bodies are usually quite good for inexpensive dolls, much better than those by companies that used a sawdust and glue mixture and didn't even paint it. This small A.M. 390 is wearing an appropriate 1920s dress and hat.
H & J Foulke, Inc.

Porzellanfabrik Mengersgereuth

This porcelain factory, known as P.M. for short, was located near Sonneberg and was a latecomer into the doll business, having opened in 1908. In 1913, it was taken over by Robert Carl, who made a line of child doll heads incised *Trebor*, which was simply "Robert" spelled backwards. The P.M. factory is not known for high quality bisque. Most of their designs are fairly ordinary.

18in (46cm) doll marked *Trebor*. This doll is seldom found. *H & J Foulke, Inc.*

Ernst Metzler

This is another small porcelain factory located in Bavaria and founded in 1909. Research has revealed that hundreds of small factories in Germany produced china and porcelain products. No one will ever know the names and details of all of them.

his doll from mold 890 by Ernst Metzler has a fairly common face of medium qual-y. She is interesting to doll collectors who like to find an unusual mark or those who e particularly looking for all original dolls. She is an inexpensive model, however, tested to by the cheap quality of the fabric used for her clothes, the glued instead sewn wig and the body with "stick legs." *H & J Foulke, Inc.*

Gebrüder Ohlhaver

Ohlhaver Brothers doll factory was founded in 1912. They purchased bisque heads from Gebrüder Heubach, Ernst Heubach and Porzellanfabrik Mengersgereuth. They registered the *Revalo* trademark, which was Ohlhaver backwards without the "h's." The character babies and child dolls with the *Revalo* mark are very good quality bisque. Perhaps it was their highest priced and best quality line.

This 17in (43cm) *Revalo* girl has a very appealing face that collectors really like. It has a little more character than an ordinary dolly face. This head was designed to have real upper eyelashes, which, as in this example, often deteriorate or fall off leaving no upper lashes at all. This does not affect the value of the doll, although some collectors prefer dolls that still have their real lashes. *Revalo* dolls are usually on very good composition and wood bodies. *H & J Foulke, Inc.*

Theodore Recknagel

The Recknagel porcelain factory was established in 1886 in Alexandrienthal, Germany. Their primary focus was on small babies and character heads.

I was very surprised when I looked at the mark on this 24in (61cm) very pretty, good quality, bisque-head doll to find that she was incised "R.A. 1909." It is the first time I had seen an R.A. doll of this large size. She would be of great interest to a collector looking for a doll that was just a little different from the ordinary. She has a replaced wig that seems a little too heavy for her. *H & J Foulke, Inc.*

Bruno Schmidt

Founded in 1898, the Bruno Schmidt doll factory in Waltershausen is well known as a producer of lovely, excellent quality character dolls, but seldom are any BSW dolly faces seen. Obviously, the factory must have primarily used unmarked heads or standard B.P. heads; it is known that Schmidt used bisque doll heads made by Bähr & Pröschild. In 1918, Schmidt purchased the B.P. factory.

This lovely 26in (66cm) dolly-face girl is marked with the "BSW" trademark o Bruno Schmidt. She has excellent bisque and a nice expression. She still retains he real original upper eyelashes. Her old wig is brown human hair, and she is on a excellent quality composition and wood jointed body. She is wearing a very appro priate plaid cotton dress with white yoke. *H & J Foulke, Inc.*

Franz Schmidt & Co.

The Franz Schmidt doll factory was also located near Waltershausen. It was founded in 1890. It is well known for character dolls but also produced dolly-faced models for 20 years prior to the issuing of character dolls. Heads were made by Simon & Halbig and J. D. Kestner (mold 293).

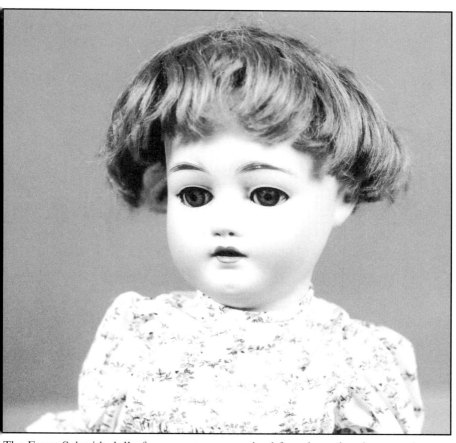

The Franz Schmidt dolly faces went unrecognized for a long time because they are incised only "S & C," but it has now been determined that this is indeed a Franz Schmidt mark. This 18in (46cm) girl has a flapper style body with high knee joint to accommodate short skirts without showing an ugly ball joint. A full-length view of her body is shown in the *9th Blue Book*, page 17. She has rubber hands. Her head was made by Simon & Halbig and has the unusual feature of pierced nostrils (often found on Schmidt character babies). She is very seldom found. Dolls with this body style of the 1920s are quite popular. *H & J Foulke, Inc.*

Peter Scherf

The Peter Scherf doll factory was founded in 1879 in Sonneberg. Some bisque heads were poured for Scherf by Armand Marseille. Although their quality is only average, the Scherf dolls are popular because of their appealing look.

A 13-1/2in (34cm) dolly face with the "P. Sch" mark of Peter Scherf. Her eyebrows are nicely painted, and her eyes are attractive. Small Scherf dolls usually have composition bodies with "stick" type legs. Many Scherf dolls are shoulder head models *H & J Foulke, Inc.*

Schoenau & Hoffmeister

Arthur Schoenau opened his doll factory in 1884 in Sonneberg. In 1901, he added a porcelain factory so that he could make complete dolls. In general, I think the Schoenau & Hoffmeister dolls have been underrated by collectors. The bisque is usually quite good and the faces are appealing. Probably the most commonly found dolly face is mold 1909, which is an attractive child. A photograph of this mold is shown in the **10th Blue Book of Dolls and Values**® on page 322. A head that I think is important, but which I have never owned or had the opportunity to photograph because I've seen only two or three, is the very well modeled one incised "*Kunstlerkopf*," which means "artist head." The bodies used by Schoenau are good but not of Waltershausen quality. The smaller dolls are on Sonneberg "stick leg" bodies, so I would avoid those. The Schoenau & Hoffmeister heads are marked with the letters "S H" on each side of a star with the letters "PB" inside. The "PB" stands for Porzellanfabrik Burggrub; the Schoenau & Hoffmeister porcelain factory was located in Burggrub, Bavaria.

This 15in (38cm) S PB H mold 4000 girl has quite a pert face. Her original wig is quite worn, but someone has made a curl at each side. Even though the wig is rather sparse, I prefer the original to a replacement. Her face is sweet, but she is on a "stick leg" body, so, if you like the face, you just have to put up with the scrappy body. *H & J Foulke, Inc.*

The lovely almond-shaped eyes on this 20in (51cm) S PB H 5800 girl are very attractive, and she has quite good bisque. Her clothes are replacements, and the dress is made of a fabric that is too new looking for my taste. I would prefer a more subdued cotton stripe, but the white aprons are appropriate on these types of dolls. *H & J Foulke, Inc.*

This 20in (51cm) S PB H 4600 has very pretty pale bisque, accented by her dark eyes, eyebrows and hair. Her full lips are nicely painted with shading strokes. *H & J Foulke, Inc.*

This 18-1/2in (31cm) S PB H 5000 ha been dressed like a boy, which provides refreshing variation to a collection and little company for the girls. This mol which has an engaging face, is not com monly found. *H & J Foulke, Inc.*

ABOVE: Left: This 22in (56cm) example of an S PB H 5500 is my personal favorite of this group. Her total appearance is engaging, including her old blonde mohair wig and her old pink and white cotton dress. *H & J Foulke, Inc.* **Right:** This 26in (66cm) doll has the name *"Pansy"* incised on the back of her head. Sometimes *Pansy* will have a Roman numeral under her name. Schoenau & Hoffmeister made some of the *Pansy* heads, but their porcelain factory mark was not used on them. Although this pictured *Pansy* has a very full face, another that I have just acquired and have not yet photographed is incised *"Pansy II"* and has a slimmer face with pale bisque. Some *Pansy* dolls have real upper eyelashes. The *Pansy* trademark was used from 1910-1922. *H & J Foulke, Inc.*

FOR FURTHER READING

BOOKS

Coleman, Dorothy S., Elizabeth Ann and Evelyn Jane.
- *The Collector's Encyclopedia of Dolls, Vol. I & II.* New York: Crown Publishers, Inc., 1968 & 1986.
- *The Collector's Book of Dolls' Clothes.* New York: Crown Publishers, Inc., 1975.

Cieslik, Jürgen and Marianne.
- *German Doll Encyclopedia 1800-1939.* Cumberland, MD: Hobby House Press, Inc., 1985.

Foulke, Jan.
- *Blue Book of Dolls & Values®. Vol. I-XII.* Grantsville, MD: Hobby House Press, Inc., 1974-1995.
- *Kestner King of Dollmakers.* Cumberland, MD: Hobby House Press, Inc., 1982.
- *Simon & Halbig Dolls.* Cumberland, MD: Hobby House Press, Inc., 1984.

ARTICLES

Foulke, Jan.
- "Bähr & Pröschild Porcelain Factory," *Doll Reader*, August 1992.
- "Armand Marseille Doll Heads," *Doll Reader*, October 1993.

Simon & Halbig

The Simon & Halbig porcelain factory opened in the Waltershausen area of Thüringia in 1869. Many collectors consider the heads poured at the S & H factory to be the finest of any German factory, not only because of their consistently high quality, but also because of their designs. In an era when some companies used the same mold for years upon years, S & H was producing a variety of models that were quite distinctive for their time. The S & H heads were made from a fine, smooth bisque with exquisite decoration and finishing. They are of the quality associated with fine porcelain figurines, not toys. Of course, as is the case in the overall German doll industry, the quality did deteriorate during the 1920s.

Simon & Halbig did not make complete dolls, except for all

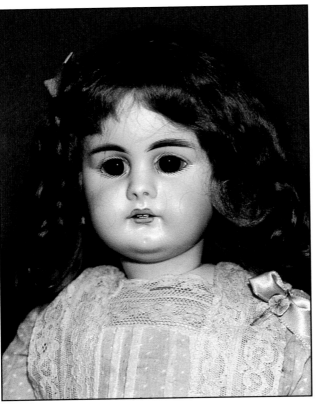

This early model of a 21in (53cm) S & H 949 girl is a true beauty. Her features are glowing; her bisque is outstanding, of the quality referred to at the time as "French" bisque even though it was made in Germany. Her full lips have shading strokes and she has desirable square cut top and bottom teeth. Like most Simon & Halbig dolls, she has pierced ears and can wear earrings, a feature enjoyed by collectors. *Jensen's Antique Dolls.*

bisque ones. They made only bisque heads and parts. They supplied numerous doll factories with heads either from S & H stock inventory or especially made from doll factory designs. Probably their most famous line was for the Kämmer & Reinhardt firm, which actually purchased the S & H factory in 1920. The quality of the S & H heads can be attested to by the fact that some French firms had heads poured by Simon & Halbig.

This 26in (66cm) S & H 1039 is an example of an early model of this mold, which dates from 1891. She has a very French look to her, with her dark glass eyes and heavy dark eyebrows. When she was new, her open mouth would have been a luxury feature, making her more expensive than a closed-mouth doll. Soon after this time, all German dollies had open mouths, so that feature was no longer expensive. Not only does this doll have a dynamite face, she also has a lovely old wig and lovely old clothes. She is a very desirable doll. *H & J Foulke, Inc.*

This 20-1/2in (52cm) girl is a shoulder head model mold 1040, which has the same face as the 1039 but in a shoulder head version. These twin faces were a consistent practice with S & H. Their socket head models ended in a "9," and their shoulder heads in a "0." The fact that this face looks so different from the 1039 shown above is because the eyes and the mouth are cut quite a bit smaller on this doll. The 1040 mold is very seldom found. *H & J Foulke, Inc.*

This 22in (56cm) girl with a saucy face is from mold 570. The 500 series, which consists of 530, 540 and 550 as well, seems to me to show faces made after 1910 because they have a hint of a character look about them. The ears are not pierced, and the lips are not shaded – two economy features. Many 550 dolls in our area are found with "Gimbel Brothers" stamped on their bodies. It was a New York and Philadelphia department store with a large doll department. Some of this series may also be found on Heinrich Handwerck bodies. The pictured doll has her original brown human hair wig with long curls and hairbows. This type of wig was a luxury item. *H & J Foulke, Inc.*

This 18in (46cm) doll is incised "S & H" and "G.S." It must have been a special order head that Simon & Halbig poured for a particular factory, possible Gebrüder Sussenguth. She has a fac very similar to the 1039 mold. Her wig is original, but her dress has been replaced. The style of the dress is correct, but I prefer older fabrics. *H & J Foulke, Inc.*

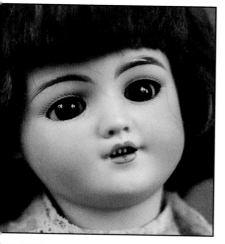

ABOVE: Left: This 18in (46cm) girl is from the 1249 mold incised *"Santa."* This is a very popular model with collectors and brings a premium price for a dolly face. Her distinguishing characteristic – besides her delightful expression – is the triangular, shaded spot on her lower lip. Sometimes the mold appears without the *"Santa,"* but it is the same face. *Santa* was made specially for Hamburger & Co., a New York importing firm, in 1900. It was advertised through 1910. The same face appears on S & H mold 1250, which is a shoulder head and presents a good opportunity for a collector to buy the *Santa* face for a lot less because kid bodied dolls are not as popular as dolls with jointed bodies. *H & J Foulke, Inc.* **Right:** Simon & Halbig made a large number of small doll heads on 5-piece composition bodies with molded socks and shoes. Small dolls are quite popular with collectors because they are easy to display and don't take up a lot of space. They are particularly charming when they are wearing their original clothes, as is this 8in (20cm) doll from mold 1079. The outfit is a very good quality white cotton with lace trim; the underclothes are complete. She has her original blonde mohair wig and a hat to match her dress. She is from mold 1079, which was introduced in 1892 but used for about 30 years. It is the most commonly found S & H head but is well worth collecting when it has special charm as this example does. *H & J Foulke, Inc.* **Bottom right:** This 22in (56cm) girl was made by Simon & Halbig for Wiesenthal, Schindel & Kallenberg, who operated a doll factory in Waltershausen, and is incised with the "WSK" initials as well. She was probably part of the *My Dearie* line of WSK dolls handled by George Borgfeldt, the New York importer, from 1908 to 1922. This doll's plus factors are her original curly blonde mohair wig with hairbows and her red piqué sailor-style dress and matching cap. *Dr. Carole Stoessel Zvonar Collection.*

Schuetzmeister & Quendt

Founded in 1889, Schuetzmeister & Quendt operated a porcelain factory that was near Waltershausen, producing bisque doll heads, bathing dolls, pincushion dolls, and knick knacks. Dolly faces with the S & Q mark are seldom found; their quality is very good. However, S & Q did make heads for Kämmer & Reinhardt after 1918.

This S & Q dolly face number 101 is 18in (46cm) tall. She has smooth bisque, an engaging face and nicely painted features. On a good quality jointed composition body, she is clearly an above average doll. *H & J Foulke, Inc.*

Unknown Manufacturers

Because I have been buying and selling dolls for so long, some of the most interesting dolls to me are the unmarked ones - the ones we look at and wonder, "Who made you? I wish you could tell us." After you have looked at dolls for a time, you begin to recognize an unusual face or an especially fine quality doll. You begin to notice their individual characteristics and can often identify a doll, or determine in which area of Germany it was made. You should not hesitate to buy an unmarked doll of quality. If "the look" is there, the doll is speaking for itself.

There are a host of other unidentifiable dolls in addition to the ones we have shown. Others with good faces and quality are marked "444," "LHK," and "182."

This 23in (58cm) doll is incised "*Princess.*" This was a trademark registered by George Borgfeldt, the gigantic New York importing firm, and used from 1897-1908. Borgfeldt not only sold dolls from established firms such as Kämmer & Reinhardt but also had factories in Germany where dolls were made. Bisque heads were made for Borgfeldt by Armand Marseille, Simon & Halbig, Kling, and Alt, Beck & Gottschalck. *H & J Foulke, Inc.*

This wide-eyed little girl is incised only "50" but is possibly by Max Rader, who apparently had a porcelain factory that made bisque heads between 1910 and 1913 in the Sonneberg area. She has a likeable face with quite a bit of individuality. When buying dolly faces, I'm always looking for one like this with a little bit of a different visage. She is 20-1/2in (52 cm) tall. *H & J Foulke, Inc.*

This 19in (48cm) girl with well modeled and decorated face is incised only "3." She is excellent quality and especially nice with her original mohair wig. Some collectors are afraid to buy a doll with no maker's name because they don't know what to pay. In this instance, you have to relate the doll to a known one. I would evaluate this doll as Simon & Halbig quality, so, if she has a good quality body, I would pay at least the same price for her and probably 20% more than I would pay for a S & H 1079 doll. After you have been involved with dolls for a while, you begin to understand that the face and quality are equally important as the mark on the back of the head. *H & Foulke, Inc.*

Although this dolly face, which is marked "23.3" with "x" and "dep," has a French aspect to her, she is a very fine German doll from an unknown manufacturer. There should be no hesitation in adding her to a doll collection. *H & J Foulke, Inc.*

This early 16in (41cm) German open-mouth girl is incised "1007x" and has good quality, pale bisque. Her plus factors are that she has lovely, gray paperweight eyes and an open mouth with upper square cut teeth, giving her quite a distinctive visage. Her old brown wig is the same color as her multi-stroked eyebrows. She has a socket head on a jointed composition and wood body. Her manufacturer has not been identified. *H & J Foulke, Inc.*

TIPS FOR COLLECTING DOLLY FACES

1. As in any other area of doll collecting, always buy the best example that you can afford.

Quality. Look for an example with smooth bisque and an even complexion. The decoration of the eyebrows, eyelashes and lips should be pleasing. Cheek tinting should be even. You may find a few minor production flaws, such as a few black specks or a molding split behind the ear. These things do not affect the value of a doll. But don't buy one which has firing splits at the eye corners or is peppered with black spots. You also have to expect that you might find slight cheek rubs or some wig pulls. Again, these don't devalue a doll, but you don't want to have half of the cheek color gone either.

"The Look." Some collectors call this "presence." It is hard to define, and it doesn't always hinge on just one attribute. Sometimes there is some special aspect that makes a doll outstanding or the best example ever seen. Sometimes this is a visual appeal and sometimes it's from the heart.

Condition. Look for a head with no cracks, chips or repairs. Small chips at the crown rim or the bottom of the neck sockets or on the bottom of the shoulder plate are no problem. Check very carefully at special areas where hairlines often occur: at the neck socket, at the eye cuts and at the crown rim. I always check my bisque doll heads by removing the wigs and shining a bright light into the head. Because the bisque is translucent, this method immediately reveals any hairlines. Repairs will show up as dark areas. You must, however, check the eye cuts for small chips or repairs because the plaster behind the eye cuts means that these areas are not translucent.

Hairlines. Whether or not to buy a doll with a hairline or damage is a matter of personal opinion and acceptance. The days of having to apologize for owning a doll with a hairline are over. There are lots of beautiful and rare dolls that have hairlines. The important thing to remember is that you don't want to pay full "book" price for a doll that doesn't have a perfect head. Many collectors feel, and rightly so, that a doll with damage provides them with an opportunity to own a particular doll that they might not be able to afford if it were in perfect condition. I think the general rule of thumb should be: stay away from a common doll with a hairline. If it's a rare doll, consider it carefully.

Body. Check to see that the head fits on the body. There should not be a large gap between the neck of the head and the collar of the body. Sometimes you will see a side gap where the neck of the body may have warped, or, on an early composition body with a wooden collar, you may not have as snug a fit as with a cardboard collar. These are not problems. The body should be in good condition of the proper type for the head, from the same factory if it is marked. All the parts should be matched; double check to see that the hands match. Repair is acceptable, but collectors do not like bodies that are totally repainted. Unfortunately, back in the 1940s and 1950s, many doll hospitals didn't know how to clean bodies and simply repainted them because they were dirty. This can be removed with paint remover – a messy job but worth the trouble. A total repaint should be examined carefully because it could be hiding parts that are replaced. On a kid body, check the arms to be sure that they match the body. It is acceptable for a kid body to have patches.

Wigs and Clothes. Whenever possible, it is best for dolls to have old wigs and clothes. I prefer the old ones even if they are worn, sparse or scraggly. Faded and patched clothes look surprisingly better if they are washed and ironed. If you have to go with new clothes, be sure that they are in styles and fabrics that compliment the dolls. Shiny new synthetics and satins and pure white laces just don't fit with old dolls. Old wigs were either human hair or mohair (hair from the angora goat). Mohair was actually better because it is softer and finer and more natural looking for a child than the coarser human hair. Lovely new mohair wigs are now available, and these are great for old dolls.

2. If you find a better example of a doll than one in your collection, you can always upgrade. Buy the better one and sell the lesser one. What would make a better example? You might find a doll with a more appealing face or one with better decoration. You might even be lucky enough to find one with outstanding original clothes.

3. Shop around for the best doll price. On some of the more common bisque-head dolls, sometimes you can get a good bargain. Always ask the dealer if there is a "better price." A dealer is not insulted if you are polite about asking. Some dealers price their dolls with the idea that they will give a discount; some dealers do not. But it doesn't hurt to ask.

4. Learn how to do minor repair work. Sometimes you can buy a good doll for less if it is unstrung, dirty and undressed. Many collectors enjoy cleaning and putting dolls together. However, be wary of buying a doll that has to go to the doll hospital because repair work on bodies can be costly. Fingers cost $10 each, for example; neck and joint work can be $20-$30, and setting eyes can run $30-$55. Repair costs can add up fast and cancel out your bargain.

5. Learn how to dress dolls appropriately. This does not necessarily mean that you need to sew the clothes yourself, although, of course, many collectors love this aspect of the hobby. Many dealers sell old clothing and wigs for the dolls that you purchased for less because they were naked. If you do want to sew for your dolls, be sure to choose old fabrics and make the clothes in appropriate styles for the dolls. Some dolls came in fancy silk dresses with large hats and look stunning in these outfits. Some look better in simple, cotton everyday dresses.

6. If you are buying at an auction, always inspect the doll before it comes up for sale. Never bid on a doll you didn't examine. It may look great from your seat five rows back, but there may be large cheek rubs or hairlines that you can't see from that distance. Also, if the doll is dressed, you can't tell anything about the age, condition or appropriateness of the body. A doll may seem as if it is selling for a cheap price until you purchase it and see all its problems!

7. Find other collectors with the same special interest as yours. Your best network for learning about the type doll you like most is other collectors and dealers. It is a lot of fun to have someone with whom to share your finds – and whose finds you can appreciate. However, you must be careful to collect what *you* like, not what your friends think you should buy. It is *your* collection and should reflect *your* tastes.

8. Read, study and enjoy your hobby!

ABOUT The Author, JAN FOULKE

The name Jan Foulke is synonymous with accurate information. As the author of the **Blue Book of Dolls & Values**®, heralded by *U.S.A. Today* as "The bible of doll collecting...", she is the most quoted source on doll information and the most respected and recognized authority on dolls and doll prices in the world.

Born in Burlington, New Jersey, Jan Foulke has always had a fondness for dolls. She recalls, "Many happy hours of my childhood were spent with dolls as companions, since we lived on a quiet county road, and until I was ten, I was an only child." Jan and her husband, Howard, who photographs the dolls presented in Jan's many titles, were both fond of antiquing as a hobby, and in 1972 they decided to open a small antique shop of their own. The interest of their daughter, Beth, in dolls sparked their curiosity about the history of old dolls – an interest that quite naturally grew out of their love of heirlooms. The stock in their antique shop gradually changed and evolved into an antique doll shop.

Early in the development of their antique doll shop, Jan and Howard realized that there was a critical need for an accurate and reliable doll identification and price guide resource. In the early 1970s, the Foulkes teamed up with Hobby House Press to produce (along with Thelma Bateman) the first **Blue Book of Dolls & Values,** originally published in 1974. Since that time, the Foulkes have exclusively authored and illustrated the eleven successive editions, which have sold over 1/2 million copies. Today the **Blue Book** is regarded by collectors and dealers as the definitive source for doll prices and values.

Jan and Howard Foulke now dedicate all of their professional time to the world of dolls: writing and illustrating books and articles, appraising collections, lecturing on antique dolls, acting as consultants to museums, auction houses and major collectors, and selling dolls both by mail order and through exhibits at major shows throughout the United States. Mrs. Foulke is a member of the United Federation of Dolls Clubs, Doll Collectors of America, and the International Doll Academy.

12th Blue Book Dolls & Values®

by Jan Foulke

You will find this classic identification and price guide book indispensable. The book features 516 photographs, 310 in color, of antique to collectible dolls. This is the guide that doll dealers use. With this book you are a doll appraiser! **#H4940 $17.95.**

"...the doll devotees bible"
The Washington Post

"The bible of doll collecting..."
U.S.A. Today

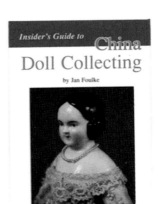
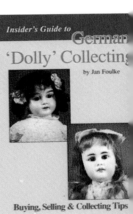